A Garland of Roses

A Garland of Roses

Edited by Gail Harvey

Gramercy Books
New York • Avenel, New Jersey

Introduction and Compilation
Copyright © 1992 by Outlet Book Company, Inc.
All rights reserved
First published in 1992 by Gramercy Books
distributed by Outlet Book Company, Inc.,
a Random House Company,
40 Engelhard Avenue
Avenel, New Jersey 07001

Manufactured in Hong Kong

Designed by Melissa Ring

Library of Congress Cataloging-in-Publication Data
A Garland of roses.
p.   cm.
ISBN 0-517-07756-6
1. Roses—Literary collections.
PN6071.R58G3   1992
820.8′036—dc20   91-39846   CIP

8 7 6 5 4 3 2 1

Introduction

$\mathcal{T}$he rose, the most popular of all flowers, exalted for its scent and its beauty, is the symbol of love and an emblem of royalty. Naturally elegant, it is regarded as the epitome of perfection. It is therefore no wonder that since ancient times the rose has been entwined in mythology and movingly portrayed in paintings and literature.

A Garland of Roses is a celebration of this exquisite

flower. It is a delightful collection of poems and prose written by some of the world's great writers, including John Keats, Christina Rossetti, Emily Dickinson, William Shakespeare, Elizabeth Barrett Browning, and Robert Burns. There are also easy-to-follow recipes for aromatic potpourris and luxurious beauty preparations.

Enchantingly illustrated, this lovely book is, indeed, a fitting tribute to the rose—the world's most revered, loved, and admired flower.

GAIL HARVEY

New York
1992

What's in a name? That which we call a rose,

By any other name would smell as sweet.

William Shakespeare

You may break, you may shatter the vase
   if you will,
But the scent of the roses will hang round
   it still.

THOMAS MOORE

A Rose is sweeter in the budde than full blowne.

John Lyly

M.E.GRAY

They're sleeping beneath the roses;
  Oh! kiss them before they rise,
And tickle their tiny noses,
  And sprinkle the dew on their eyes.
    Make haste, make haste;
    The fairies are caught;
      Make haste.

WILLIAM CORY

$\mathcal{Q}$ueen of fragrance, lovely rose,
The beauties of thy leaves disclose!
The Winter's past, the tempests fly,
Soft gales breathe gently through the sky;
The lark sweet warbling on the wing
Salutes the gay return of spring:
The silver dews, the vernal showers,
Call forth a bloomy waste of flowers;
The joyous fields, the shady woods,
Are cloth'd with green, or swell with buds;
Then haste thy beauties to disclose,
Queen of fragrance, lovely rose!

WILLIAM BROOME

Then, then, in strange eventful hour,
The earth produced an infant flower,
Which sprung with blushing tinctures drest,
And wantoned o'er its parent's breast.
The gods beheld this brilliant birth,
And hailed the Rose, the boon of earth.

THOMAS MOORE

*T*he lily has an air,
 And the snowdrop a grace,
And the sweet-pea a way,
 And the heart's-ease a face,—
Yet there's nothing like the rose
 When she blows.

CHRISTINA G. ROSSETTI

G<small>O</small>, lovely rose,
Tell her, that wastes her time and me,
That now she knows,
When I resemble her to thee,
How sweet and fair she seems to be.

E<small>DMUND</small> W<small>ALLER</small>

*I*f love were what the rose is,
  And I were like the leaf,
Our lives would grow together
In sad or singing weather,
Blown fields or flowerful closes,
  Green pleasure or gray grief;
If love were what the rose is,
  And I were like the leaf.

ALGERNON SWINBURNE

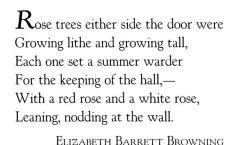

Rose trees either side the door were
Growing lithe and growing tall,
Each one set a summer warder
For the keeping of the hall,—
With a red rose and a white rose,
Leaning, nodding at the wall.

ELIZABETH BARRETT BROWNING

Roses at first were white,
    Till they could not agree,
Whether my Sappho's breast,
    Or they more white should be.

But being vanquished quite,
    A blush their cheeks be-spread;
Since which (believe the rest)
    The Roses first came red.

ROBERT HERRICK

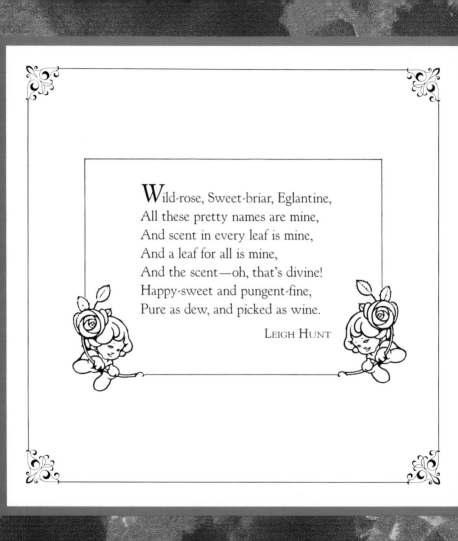

Wild-rose, Sweet-briar, Eglantine,
All these pretty names are mine,
And scent in every leaf is mine,
And a leaf for all is mine,
And the scent—oh, that's divine!
Happy-sweet and pungent-fine,
Pure as dew, and picked as wine.

LEIGH HUNT

The rose is fairest when 't is budding new,
    And hope is brightest when it dawns from
        fears;
The rose is sweetest washed with morning dew,
    And love is loveliest when embalmed in tears.
O wilding rose, whom fancy thus endears,
    I bid your blossoms in my bonnet wave,
Emblem of hope and love through future years!

SIR WALTER SCOTT

O my Luve's like a red, red rose
  That's newly sprung in June:
O my Luve's like the melodie
  That's sweetly played in tune.
As fair art thou, my bonnie lass,
  So deep in luve am I:
And I will luve thee still, my dear,
  Till a' the seas gang dry.

ROBERT BURNS

Lately on yonder swelling bush
Big with many a coming rose,
This early bud began to blush,
And did but half itself disclose;
    I plucked it, though no better grown,
    And now you see how full 'tis blown.

EDMUND WALLER

There is an angel that abides
  Within the budding rose;
That is his home, and there he hides
  His head in calm repose.

The rosebud is his humble home,
  And there he often loves to roam;
And wending through the path of Heaven,
  Empurples all the track of even.

If e'en he sees a maiden meek,
  He hovers nigh, and flings
Upon the modest maiden's cheek
  The shadow of his wings.

Oh, lovely maiden, dost thou know
  Why thy cheeks so warmly glow?
'Tis the Angel of the Rose,
  That salutes thee as he goes.

HARTLEY COLERIDGE

Won't you come into the garden?

I would like my roses to see you.

Richard Brinsley Sheridan

Howard Chandler Christy. 1915

The red rose whispers of passion
And the white rose breathes of love.
O the red rose is a falcon
And the white rose is a dove.

JOHN B. O'REILLY

And the roses—the roses! Rising out of the grass, tangled round the sundial, wreathing the tree trunks and hanging from their branches, climbing up the walls and spreading over them with long garlands falling in cascades—they came alive day by day, hour by hour. Fair fresh leaves, and buds—and buds—tiny at first but swelling and working Magic until they burst and unclurled into cups of scent delicately spilling themselves over their brims and filling the garden air.

From *The Secret Garden*
by Frances Hodgson Burnett

ROSE GARDEN POTPOURRI

This traditional rose potpourri has a delicate, sweet yet spicy scent. Rose petals and rosebuds can be dried on a tray or fine-mesh screen in a warm, dry closet or attic.

4 cups dried rose petals
1 cup dried whole rosebuds
1 cup dried lavender flowers
1 tablespoon crushed dried orange peel
1 tablespoon ground cinnamon
1 tablespoon allspice
1 tablespoon grated nutmeg
2 tablespoons cloves
3 tablespoons orris root powder
6 drops rose oil.

In a large bowl combine all the ingredients and mix well. Transfer the potpourri to a paper bag. Seal it tightly and store in a cool, dark place for six weeks, shaking the bag occasionally.

Display the potpourri in pretty open bowls or small lined baskets.

ROSE PETAL DELIGHT

This is the easiest of potpourris to make. The rose petals are dried only until they feel dry on the surface and are still flexible. Then they are matured with other ingredients in a sealed jar. This potpourri is best kept in pretty closed containers which can be opened whenever you want their scent to perfume a room.

3 cups half-dried red rose petals
½ cup fine sea salt
grated rind of 1 large orange
1 tablespoon crushed juniper berries
4 tablespoons powdered orris root
1 tablespoon gum benzoin powder

In a large bowl combine all the ingredients and mix well. Pour the mixture into a large jar. Cover with a tightly fitting lid. Store the jar in a cool, dark place for three weeks. Before transferring the potpourri to individual containers, mix it well with a wooden spoon.

ROSE HAND CREAM

This rich moisturizing cream is easy to make from natural ingredients. The rose petals and oil add a lovely scent.

>   *2 tablespoons fresh rose petals*
>   *4 tablespoons almond oil*
>   *8 tablespoons lanolin*
>   *4 tablespoons glycerin*
>   *3 drops rose oil*

Put the rose petals into a small bowl. Add just enough boiling water to cover. Set aside to cool.

In the top of a double boiler, combine the almond oil, lanolin, and glycerin. Cook over hot water, stirring constantly, until the lanolin has melted. Pour the mixture into a food processor.

Drain the rose petals and add them to the mixture in the food processor along with the rose oil. Process at high speed until the mixture is well blended.

Pour into small glass jars and cover tightly.

ROSE WATER

In an open glass bottle, rose water will delightfully scent a bathroom. It can be used as cologne, although it is less heavily scented, or use it to perfume bath water. The rose petals will tint the water, so it looks lovely stored in clear glass bottles, perhaps with a few petals floating in it.

2 cups distilled water
½ cup vodka
1 cup fresh red rose petals
20 drops rose oil

In a large, clean wide-mouthed jar combine the distilled water and vodka. Add the rose petals and mix gently with a wooden spoon until they are thoroughly wet. Add the oil and mix gently but well.

Cover the jar tightly and put it in a cool, dark place for 1 week. This will permit the scent to age.

Strain the rose water into clean bottles. If desired, one or two fresh rose petals can be added to each bottle.

The new Rose Garden promises complete success. Caroline Testout is coming out, fat and pink and smiling in her usual good-humoured profusion. She keeps up her self-contained smile unimpaired in fair and foul weather, "fat-faced Puss" that she is, a very Gioconda among roses, even to the close folding of her plump leaves, which remind one of that over-rated charmer's compact hands. It would take a good deal to shake her equanimity; scentless, soulless beauty!

From *Our Sentimental Garden*
by Agnes and Egerton Castle

ASKING FOR ROSES

A house that lacks, seemingly, mistress and master,
  With doors that none but the wind ever closes,
Its floor all littered with glass and with plaster;
  It stands in a garden of old-fashioned roses.

I pass by that way in the gloaming with Mary;
  "I wonder," I say, "who the owner of those is."
"Oh, no one you know," she answers me airy,
  "But one we must ask if we want any roses."

So we must join hands in the dew coming coldly
 There in the hush of the wood that reposes,
And turn and go up to the open door boldly,
 And knock to the echoes as beggars for roses.

"Pray, are you within there, Mistress Who-were-you?"
 'Tis Mary that speaks and our errand discloses.
"Pray, are you within there? Bestir you, bestir you!
 'Tis summer again; there's two come for roses.

"A word with you, that of the singer recalling—
 Old Herrick: a saying that every maid knows is
A flower unplucked is but left to the falling,
 And nothing is gained by not gathering roses."

We do not loosen our hands' intertwining
 (Not caring so very much what she supposes),
There when she comes on us mistily shining
 And grants us by silence the boon of her roses.

ROBERT FROST

The rose upon my balcony the morning air
perfuming,
Was leafless all the winter time and pining
for the spring.

WILLIAM MAKEPEACE THACKERAY

Accept
this rose from a fond
heart faithful and true.

The sweetest flower that blows
I give you as we part;
For you it is a rose
For me it is my heart.

FREDERICK PETERSON

*I*t was not in the winter
Our loving was cast!
It was the time of roses,
We plucked them as we passed!

THOMAS HOOD

Marriage is like life in this—

that it is a field of battle, and not

a bed of roses.

Robert Louis Stevenson

Read in these roses the sad story
Of my hard fate, and your own glory.
 In the white you may discover
 The paleness of a fainting lover;
In the red the flames still feeding
On my heart, with fresh wounds bleeding.
 The white will tell you how I languish,
 And the red express my anguish;
The white my innocence displaying,
The red my martyrdom betraying.
 The frowns that on your brow resided,
 Have those roses thus divided.
Oh! let your smiles but clear the weather,
And then they both shall grow together.

Thomas Carew

TO A FRIEND WHO SENT ME
SOME ROSES

As late I rambled in the happy fields,
   What time the skylark shakes the tremulous dew
   From his lush clover covert;—when anew
Adventurous knights take up their dinted shields:
I saw the sweetest flower wild nature yields,
   A fresh-blown musk rose; 'twas the first that threw
   Its sweets upon the summer: graceful it grew
As is the wand that queen Titania wields.
And, as I feasted on its fragrancy:
   I thought the garden rose it far excell'd:
But when, O Wells! thy roses came to me
   My sense with their deliciousness was spell'd:
Soft voices had they, that with tender plea
   Whisper'd of peace, and truth, and friendliness
         unquell'd.

JOHN KEATS

The young rose I give thee, so dewy and bright,
Was the flow'ret most dear to the sweet bird of night,
Who oft, by the moon, o'er her blushes hath hung,
And thrilled every leaf with the wild lay he sung.

Oh, take thou this young rose, and let her life be
Prolonged by the breath she will borrow from thee;
For, while o'er her bosom thy soft notes shall thrill,
She'll think the sweet night-bird is courting her still.

THOMAS MOORE

*O*n Richmond Hill there lived a lass
More bright than May-day morn;
Whose smiles all other maids' surpass,
A rose without a thorn.

LEONARD MCNALLY

Love is like a rose, the joy of all the earth. . . .

Christina Rossetti

*L*ook, Delia, how we 'steem the half-blown rose,
The image of thy blush and Summer's honor,
Whilst in her tender green she doth inclose
That pure, sweet beauty Time bestows upon her.
No sooner spreads her glory to the air,
But straight her full-blown pride is in declining;
She then is scorned that late adorned the fair:
So clouds thy beauty, after fairest shining.
No April can revive thy withered flowers,
Whose blooming grace adorns thy glory now;
Swift, speedy Time, feathered with flying hours,
Dissolves the beauty of the fairest brow.
   Oh, let not then such riches waste in vain,
   But love, whilst that thou may'st be loved again.

SAMUEL DANIEL

Sweet rose, whence is this hue
Which doth all hues excel?
Whence this most fragrant smell,
And whence this form and gracing grace in you?
In flow'ry Paestum's field perhaps ye grew,
Or Hybla's hills you bred,
Or odoriferous Enna's plains you fed,
Or Tmolus, or where boar young Adon slew;
Or hath the queen of love you dyed of new
In that dear blood, which makes you look so red?
   No, none of those, but cause more high you blest,
   My lady's breast you bare, and lips you kissed.

WILLIAM DRUMMOND

A Rose, as fair as ever saw the North,
Grew in a little garden all alone;
A sweeter flower did Nature ne'er put forth,
Nor fairer garden yet was never known.
And maidens danced about it more and more,
And learned bards of it their ditties made;
The nimble Fairies, by the pale-faced moon,
Watered the roots, and kissed her pretty shade.
But well-a-day, the gard'ner careless grew;
The maids and Fairies both were kept away,
And in a drought the caterpillars threw
Themselves upon the bud and every spray:
    God shield the stock! if Heaven send no supplies,
    The fairest blossom of the garden dies.

WILLIAM BROWNE

'Tis the last rose of summer,
Left blooming alone;
All her lovely companions
Are faded and gone.

THOMAS MOORE

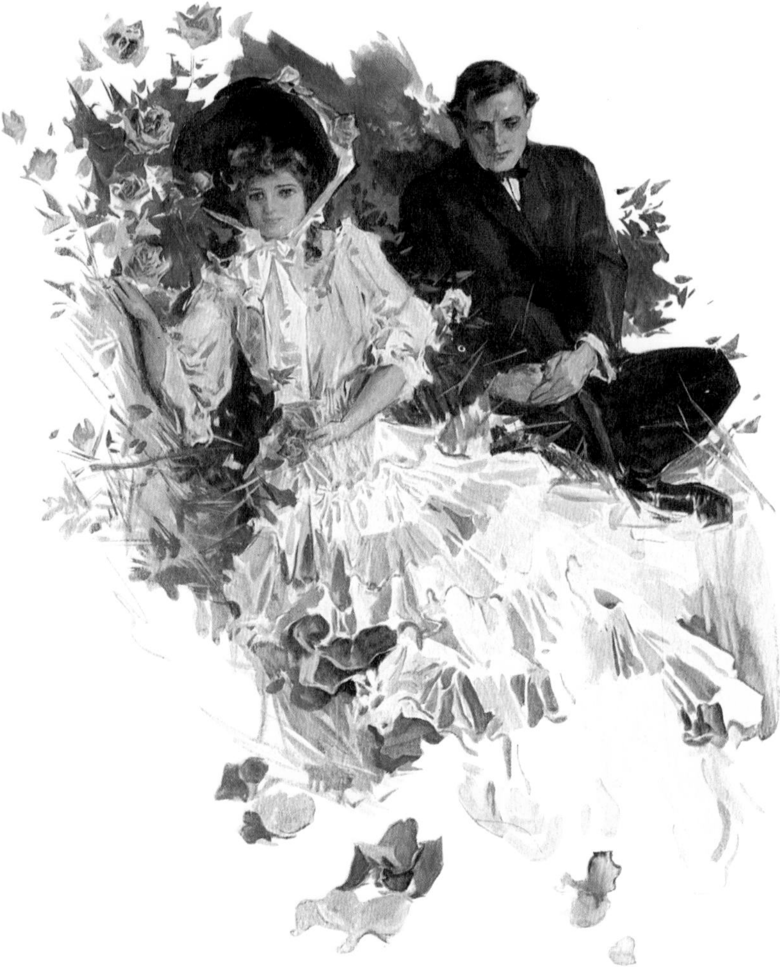

$\mathcal{N}$obody knows this little rose,
It might a pilgrim be,
Did I not take it from the ways,
And lift it up to thee.

Only a bee will miss it,
Only a butterfly,
Hastening from far journey
On its breast to lie;

Only a bird will wonder,
Only a breeze will sigh;
Ah! little rose, how easy
For such as thee to die!

EMILY DICKINSON

Gather ye rosebuds while ye may,
 Old Time is still a-flying;
And this same flower that smiles today,
 Tomorrow will be dying.

ROBERT HERRICK